Thread Me a Button

Thread Me a Button

**Jude Aquilina
& Joan Fenney**

For my mother,
Joan, who sat on my bed
countless times as we emptied
the button tin and talked
about anything.
Jude

For Lynette and Sarah
the creative threads in my life
who inspire me with their talent
and generosity.
Joan

Thread Me a Button
ISBN 978 1 74027 733 4
Copyright © text Jude Aquilina and Joan Fenney 2012
Illustrations by Sarah John
Cover design by Joan Fenney

First published 2012
Reprinted 2016

Ginninderra Press
PO Box 3461 Port Adelaide SA 5015
www.ginninderrapress.com.au

Contents

Foreword	7
Buttons defined	8
In the sewing drawer	9
At our fingertips	11
Mother's collection	12
Sacred	13
How do fingers sense	14
Spare buttons	15
Seamstress	16
Beginner	17
In the light	18
Haberdashery dreaming	20
Love's tangled thread	**21**
Climbing back	23
A common thread	24
From her lover's uniform	26
Buttoned against sin	27
Nipples	28
Love's promise	29
Dark holes	**33**
Haiku	35
Deep in a forest	36
In shadows	37
Stories from remnants	38
Memento	39
Don't curse your cardie	40
The fat aftermath	41
Lunar cat	43
I heard a strange tale…	44
the button that has worried us…*	45

A buttonhole to history — 47

Museum of Lost Buttons — 49
Famous buttons — 51
Relic of faith — 52
Still life — 53
Bizarre buttons — 54
A lady's cuffs — 55
Boutons fantaisie — 56
Enigma — 57
Might come in handy — 58

Of kith and kin — 59

Puppeteer — 61
Together — 62
Ruby's red coat — 63
Broken toys — 65
Bellybuttons — 66
It's a boy — 67
Bob Ellis's top button — 68
When Piggy caught his lily — 69

by Jude — 70
by Joan — 70
Acknowledgements — 71

Foreword

'Buttons should be bold, brilliant, basic or beautiful, but never, never boring.' – Joyce Whittemore

Join us on a journey of exploration, from the humble origins of buttons as ornaments and fabric fasteners, to the many meanings the word has morphed into. Since buttons first appeared in ancient times they have been traded, admired as status symbols, sealed with secrets, pressed for war, collected, carved, and crafted by designers. Buttons have their own unique stories and have been held by hands from all ages.

Our mutual love of buttons began when we were young and first rattled our grandmothers' button tins and so we embarked on a project to write poems about these brilliant little inventions: from grandfathers' leather buttons, button eyes on toys, buttons on trouser flies, baby clothes and wedding dresses, to bellybuttons, button mushrooms and buttons that determine the future of the world. People's passion for buttons extends worldwide, resulting in button shops, blogs, societies, conventions and fairs.

We thank those who have generously given us inspiration in the form of button gifts or stories. The thread between button lovers is indeed strong. Even if you're not a button collector, you'll discover memories, magic and humour in these poems.

Buttons defined

button *n & v n.* **1** a small disc or knob sewn on to a garment, either to fasten it by being pushed through a buttonhole, or as an ornament or badge. **2** a knob on a piece of esp. electronic equipment which is pressed to operate it. **3 a** a small round object *(chocolate buttons).* **b** *(attrib)* anything resembling a button *(button nose).* **4 a** a bud. **b** a button mushroom. **5** *Fencing* a terminal knob on a foil making it harmless. *v.* **1** *tr. & intr.* = *button up* 1. **2** *tr.* supply with buttons. ¤ **buttonball tree** (or **button wood**) *US* a plane tree, *Platanus accidentalis*. **button chrysanthemum** a variety of chrysanthemum with small spherical flowers. **button-down** applied to a collar whose points are buttoned to the shirt. **buttoned up** *colloq.* **1** formal and inhibited in manner. **2** silent. **button grass 1** the large tufted sedge *Gymnoschoenus sphaerocephalus*, bearing button-like flowers on tall thin stalks and forming distinctive plains, esp. in western Tasmania. **2** the short-lived annual grass *Dactyloctenium radulans* of mainland Australia. **button one's lip** *colloq.* remain silent. **button mushroom** a young unopened mushroom. **button quail** any of several quail-like Australian birds of the genus *Turnix* (related to the true quail of Australia, but smaller in size and lacking a hind toe). **button-through** (of a dress) fastened with buttons from neck to hem like a coat. **button up 1** fasten with buttons. **2** *colloq.* complete (a task etc.) satisfactorily. **3** *colloq.* become silent. **not worth a button** worthless. ¤¤ **buttoned** *adj.* **buttonless** *adj. buttony adj.* [Middle English from old French *bouton*, ultimately from Germanic]

From *The Australian Concise Oxford Dictionary*, Fourth Edition, edited by Bruce Moore at the Australian National Dictionary Centre, Oxford University Press, 2004

In the sewing drawer

a lifetime of buttons

At our fingertips

Buttons –
hanging by a thread
stitched with love
holding treasures
sealed with secrets
pressed for war
carved by hand
falling from sky
whimsical, sacred
lost and found.
A lifetime of buttons
at our fingertips.

Mother's collection

for Joan Lockier

The tartan plaid biscuit tin rattles like rain as I walk.
A cloth is spread on the double bed and buttons hail,
strange little pebbles to be sifted and slowly sorted.
After a while my eyes magnify and I'm in tiny town
where marcasite greys sparkle silver, and I must rub
the brown pretzel knots of leather jacket buttons;
hold mother-of-pearl to light and see rainbow ripples.
Rivalry between my children over who'll find the button
Mum likes best and sheer elation if I sew it to a garment.

Sometimes I go back through a buttonhole to my childhood
these inherited buttons hold a chestful of memories
when my mother and I sat and plunged our fingers in.
Occasionally the bite of a hidden needle and I'd wait
for the red bubble. Two holes; four holes; all the little extras:
a crystal bead, a miniature cowry shell, bra hooks.
That soldier's button with the dented emblem –
Was he saved by this tiny shield? Two holes? Four holes?
My mother lived through the Depression, kept every zip,
strap, eyelet: unusable, but safe in this poet's hands.
So again I marvel at these sewer's jewels
and fasten a few more memories onto my own children.

Sacred

Lily found

five royal blue buttons

with navy cotton still threaded

through   the four holes   shaped

strongly   by bold hands   thought

to belong to one of the ten nuns

who lived behind veils

of silence.

How do fingers sense

to push the blind needle
up through fabric
to find the target hole
again and again
as if an inner eye
guides the thread
till cotton fills
the button's empty wells?

Spare buttons

On the inside
kept in the dark
they wait in vain
to reach the other side
like mistresses
coveting the front position
who know a loss
will need to occur
for them to be stitched
to their desired place.

Seamstress

for Sarah

She collects cards of old buttons.
Nowadays they come in plastic jars,
but once they were stitched to a
piece of brown cardboard which bore
the button manufacturer's brand name.
In the drawer of her old Singer lie wooden
cotton reels and dented metal thimbles.

Holding a marquisette button to the light,
she recalls the red cape she cut it from.
Inside a jar, clear glass buttons rattle
like rain. Her Husqvarna is an extra
hand, fabric gliding between fingers and needle
as garments take shape like clouds of mist
around the table and her dainty feet.

She stitches sequins, pearls and ribbons
to complete the dream. The hum of her machine
is like insect buzz, as green rayon moves at river's pace
and all the while she's bathed in an aura
of serenity as she tunes into the muse
of pleats and gowns for kings and queens.

Beginner

The first time you showed me
how to sew a button
on my doll's pink dress
I watched your fingers
dip up and down
the needle passing through the fabric
in slow, gentle waves.
When you handed the needle to me
I tried to grasp it
but it slipped and pricked my finger
a spot of blood staining the cotton fabric.

In the light

In the shadowy light
Mrs Morris dashed
along the tree-lined street
to the pale blue walls
of *Pearl Buttons*.

In the faint glow of morning
spools of ribbon
formed rainbows across
the polished oak
beside tall jars with faded lids
brimming with buttons.

In the sharp rays of late morning
Mrs Morris cut red satin ribbon
weaving it over and under
her slender fingers.
She placed it above
the boxes of threads
with names so exotic
she only whispered them alone.

In the piercing midday sun
she pressed her hands
to her pale powdered face

and placed a thin strand
of tightly permed hair
the colour of autumn
behind her ear.
A faint scent of Lily of the Valley
crept from her blouse.

In the fierce afternoon glare
Mrs Morris opened a letter.
The only words she read were
'*to be demolished*'.
Lines circled her eyes
and tears formed droplets
like small crystal buttons
on her wooden counter.

In the faded light of dusk
Pearl Buttons was vacant.
In the window
next to an empty jar
was a small handwritten sign:

> *Last button sold.*
> *Pearl M. Morris*
> *16.2.1968*

Haberdashery dreaming

for Joan Fenney

As the shop doorbell tingles behind her
she gapes and gasps at glass counters
like a child of the desert
first meeting the sea – she breathes in
the scent of sewing machine oil
and wooden floorboards.

Joan has a passion
for cotton reels and press studs
for cards of coloured buttons,
for buckles, bobbins and pincushions,
for thimbles, needles and ribbons.

She surveys the shop
like a ship's captain
looking to moor
and dive in at the first sight
of pearl buttons.

Love's tangled thread

hanging by a thread

Climbing back

When your life
is hanging by a thread
may there be
a sturdy button
dangling there
so your feet can rest
– a plateau to stop
you slipping any further.

Let me be that button
and slowly
we will swing
wide and high,
a pendulum
rising back
to ground
where you will
again sew
crops of dreams.

A common thread

1.
In the crispness of autumn
your pram crunches
the crinkled leaves.
Buttoned for warmth
in a lavender jacket
you close your eyes
as leaves fall
around us.

At the school gate
you meet me
breathless
one sock down
buttons undone
hug my legs
we walk home
your love held
in my hand.

I hear the key turn
you rush to your room
I glimpse
teenage longing –
ruffled hair
flushed face
buttons awry
but you are home
I breathe again.

2.
The day my mother died
I wrapped myself
in her cardigan
clenched the top button
in my right hand
tried to hold onto her
as night
closed around me.

3.
Pa shuffles to the door
wearing Gran's blue cardigan
one button remains
hanging by a scarlet thread
he hands me a needle
to fasten the thread
of his ties to the past.

From her lover's uniform

Before he left for the trenches
Aunty Fay snipped a button
from her lover's uniform
stitched it to her petticoat
and waited.
He was 20, she was 19.

When the telegram came
she didn't open it
knew what it said.

Ten years later
she married a farmer
had six children in seven years
but the button stayed with her
stitched to a new petticoat
when the old one wore out.

Buttoned against sin

A button left undone:
seduction's half won.
A button sewed back
holds modesty on track.

Nipples

Nipples are not on–off buttons
they are radio dials waiting to tune in.
Nipples are not raisins
they are glacé cherries on frosted cupcakes.
Nipples are not freckles
they are beauty spots on powdered cheeks.
Nipples are not pebbles
they are lustrous pearls glistening in the shower.
Nipples are not shy
they are brave sherpas leading women on journeys.

Love's promise

If you've got an itch, I'll scratch it
with my mouth
if you've an urge to kiss, I'll match it
with my mouth
if your button pops, I'll catch it
with my mouth.

The Coles Girl

G.J. Coles Dance, 15 June 1950, Port Adelaide Town Hall

She wore a frock of red polka dots with red ribbon
threaded through her fair hair.

She didn't see me, she was with friends.
I'd left my mates back at the wharf.

My skin still crusted with salt
could never be scrubbed clean.

I wanted to run and hold her but walked slowly,
wiped the sweat from my hands.

Her voice was soft and she paused often.
I think I smelled violets.

I waited and moved closer, not wanting
to scare her.

I said my name was Bill and asked her to
dance. She nodded and lowered her eyes.

Her name was Lily and we moved
to the dance floor. I don't remember the dance.

She was a Coles girl, working with threads
and ribbons, buttons and wool. She was 19, I was 21.

I wanted to say so much but said so little.
Once she turned and her hair brushed my lips.

We danced till I found my words,
people moved around us in a slow whirl.

I hid my watch in my pocket, wanted to believe
in forever.

Lily no longer remembers our days,
but she's held my hand every night for sixty years.

Dark holes

button moon

Haiku

A button moon hangs
on a silver thread of cloud.
Aeroplane scissors.

Deep in a forest

Even without ears, she heard the birds
over the years, felt the sun thaw frost
and saw the swaying dance of
the river red gum, its roots deep,
till one wet spring when the tree toppled
and sent its huge root ball skywards.

Twisted stick in hand, the bushwalker
sees the towering mushroom of dirt and wood,
goes for a closer look and down in the crater
sees a quartz-white skull and bones
and four red buttons: little dirt-encrusted beacons
signalling the end of hope for a family somewhere.

In shadows

Smugglers' buttons held gold;
spies' buttons, cyanide –
secret little cells for when
all else was stripped.
Please let me keep
my coat for the cold,
the prisoner begged.

And the brass cuff studs,
sharp and laced with poison –
one scratch in passing
removes human thorns
from bourgeois sides.

During times of war
when no silver coins
could be found in the village
they closed the eyes
of the dead
with blessed buttons.

Stories from remnants*

Rainbows of colour
spill onto the carpet
from buckets of buttons.
Nimble fingers sift
shapes of glass and metal
plastic and wood
like miners searching for gold.
Fossicking for stories
of the Holocaust
through buttons collected
from the camps
or from the frayed
clothes of survivors.
The young girls of Israel
want to understand.

*A group of Year 8 girls, trying to comprehend the Holocaust, collected buttons and stories for the Lost Buttons Project that grew to involve schools across Israel.

Memento

memory buttons

Forever under glass
a lock of hair to hold close
a lover's keepsake.

Don't curse your cardie

Every bit as nasty
as strolling beneath a ladder
dropping a mirror or
tripping over black cats
is the curse of buttoning-up
on the wrong holes –
some say the only way
to halt the pain
of a luckless day
is to strip naked
and dress again.

The fat aftermath

And when the renegade fat people
took to the streets because no one would rent
them rooms or houses and they were forbidden
to study or work unless they underwent
'Government Buttoning',
they opened sly bakeries and lolly shops
imported chocolate
from Africa on the black market
grew illicit sugar cane in National Parks
and set up underground confectionery cells
stocked long before prohibition.

The Fat Police hunted them like dogs,
loading them into glass-sided vehicles
for all to see as they shunted them
through city streets to the nearest clinic.
Jaw wiring and stomach stapling were outlawed
years before: the community outraged at the
waste of government funds spent on hopeless
freaks, who didn't want to help themselves.

Government buttoning only requires a local anaesthetic,
a small slit in the upper lip, and a flesh-
coloured knob sewn to the inside
of the lower. Laser-sealed, the sinful
mouth is mute. The official Reduction Nurse
appears every day with a protein shake
and a long thin straw to insert through the nose.
The taste buds die after a few years and staying
within the legal range of size 0 to 1 is easy.

Lunar cat

The luminous amber buttons
of the cat's eyes
flash at midnight, fastening
a long lighthouse gaze
on the mother-of-pearl
moon floating gently
in her sea of rippled cloud.

I heard a strange tale...

One New Year's Day people reported that a bright flash
appeared in the sky; cars stopped, people stared
then a button appeared in a crack on the pavement
on the corner of 32nd Street and Park Avenue,
New York.

It was a triangular green button pierced with two holes
with a map that glowed in the dark on the back.
People gazed at the sky for a clue, puzzled over the map,
searched into the night for more buttons. None were ever
found.

Over the years the green button was passed from hand
to hand, photographed, X-rayed, scraped, probed
but no one could explain why a button would fall
from the sky.

In time people forgot about the button. Now it gathers
dust in a government office next to a file marked
'Open'.

the button that has worried us…*

Little did we know
the innocent word *button*
would hold powers
so immense
that a time might come
when a single press
could leave
a million or more
dead.

* 'When it comes to the button that has worried us the most over the years – the one that would unleash nuclear destruction – today we take another step to ensure that it will never be pushed.' – Hillary Clinton launching a landmark nuclear arms reduction pact with Russia; *The Australian*, 7 February 2011.

A buttonhole to history

Saul the storyteller of lost buttons

Museum of Lost Buttons

Each day at 6 a.m. Saul Marchant hobbles
through the cathedral arcade
of the deco building
rides the creaking lift
to the fifth floor
and unlocks the heavy iron door
to his Museum of Lost Buttons.

Down long narrow corridors
dusty shelves hold myriads
of buttons in dented glass cases.
Buttons of pearl, metal, pewter,
and glass, some beaded, others
enamelled or embossed.

Buttons from wedding dresses,
ball gowns, coats, cardigans,
jackets, gloves, boots, babies
clothes. Remnants from past lives.

Saul searches streets, laneways,
dance halls, theatres, cinemas,
cafés, churches, playing fields
gardens around the city
for lost buttons, always
carrying his battered tobacco tin.

Saul hopes to reunite buttons
with their owners and pass
on the tales of where he found them.

Few people visit the museum.
Saul the storyteller of lost buttons
waits each day for someone to claim
their missing button.

Famous buttons

Coco Chanel
made the little black dress
incomplete without a glint
of diamante button.

Carmen Miranda
transformed buttons
into fruit salad
luring many a hungry man.

Roosevelt's
teddy bear buttons
forsook hibernation
to adorn his winter suits.

Queen Victoria
caused death's jet buttons
to darken haberdashery stores
around the world.

And Louis XIV's
button lust saw him amass
enough to pave
the streets of Paris.

Relic of faith

metal button circa 14th century

Buried deep
by the Thames
from the age
of adversity
a relic of faith
with a figure
seen faintly
hands held in prayer
in a circle of light
unearthed from the past.

Still life

habitat buttons 18th century France

Captured under glass
relics from nature –
flowers, twigs, grasses,
shells, insects –
still life from
the Age of Enlightenment
stitched to the finest fabrics.

Bizarre buttons

Only a crazy tailor makes buttons
from peanuts, snails or piglet tails
from fish eyes, grapes or fingernails
from ladybird wings or lizard tongues
from beaks of ducks or dried-up dung
from mud balls, meatballs or hailstones
toadstools, slugs or jellyfish bones.

A lady's cuffs

from *Picnic at Hanging Rock**

Creamy pearl buttons
on the French lace sleeve
of the Mademoiselle
catch the morning sun
as she pours English tea from fine china,
checks her silver filigree watch,
soon to stop at twelve noon.

The rock is hot, the air still
as a strange red cloud moves
to the notes of a flute
casts a shadow on
the picnicking girls,
in their long white frocks,
from Mrs Appleyard's finishing school.

* A novel by Joan Lindsay

Boutons fantaisie

*for Elsa Schiaperelli**

In her surreal world of the 30s
she teased and amused
an adoring public
with buttons she created –
whimsical and playful
ornate and intricate:
plumed, prancing horses
that could have stepped off
a carousel
dancing clowns and acrobats
butterflies, bees and ladybugs
cupids adorned with love.
With a wave of her hand
she bade '*bonne journée*'
as the Mademoiselles paraded
along Parisian streets
in her button embellished garments.
to gasps of '*magnifique!*'

* Italian-born designer, Elsa Schiaperelli, 1890–1973, was the first person to create and use fanciful buttons. She resided and worked in Paris for most of her life.

Enigma

rebus button from 18th century France

With letters and words
a cryptic message
inscribed with love
preserved on a button –
Elle aime sans detour*

* She loves without detour.

Might come in handy

No one thrills at finding a piece of string
a paper clip or a button any more,
not even a small silver coin is worth
stooping for. Our bins and dumps
overflow with things that once
our grandparents would have saved.
Archaeologists of the future
will no longer have to dig –
there'll be man-made mountains to climb.

Of kith and kin

her sock puppets all called Pearlie

Puppeteer

My Nana searched thrift shops
for odd buttons
combed tins and jars
for blue and red shiny ones
to add to Pa's old socks –
two buttons for eyes
one for a nose
her hand for the mouth.
Her sock puppets
all called Pearlie
peeped out from corners
to lighten our days
during bleak winters
at our home
by the buffeted coast.

Together

Side by side they worked
on a cardigan for my birthday
my mother knitted the black mohair wool
my sister crafted buttons from black clay
with flecks of pink and blue,
for days they worked
heads almost touching
hands close
never appearing to stop,
a spider could have woven
a web around them.

Ruby's red coat

My sister Ruby wanted her own red coat, not my old blue one. She wanted it to be red like the cherries she hung over her ears. She wanted it to have big red buttons with dark red stitching on the collar. She wanted to be able to read the label.

We never had new coats. My mum said we were lucky to have any at all, said the cost of a new coat would feed us for a month.

Ruby cut out pictures of red coats and stuck them everywhere, left red coat reminder notes on the table. Every time she sat quietly on the couch, she said she was dreaming of her new red coat. I even heard her add a red coat plea to her night-time prayers.

One day Mum came home with a crinkled brown paper bag and gave it proudly to Ruby. Ruby pulled out a pale red coat with small black buttons and a faded label.

Ruby folded the coat back into the bag and sat with it
on her lap. Later she placed it on the floor by her bed.
I heard Mum sigh every time she passed our bedroom.
I secretly willed Ruby to try it on. As winter neared
the bag became a silent reminder of lost dreams.

On a chilly July night I crawled into bed and noticed
a pale red sleeve poking out of the covers. My sister Ruby
bundled in warmth, wrapped in love.

Broken toys

Vicki told us…

I sucked the eye off my teddy; remember
spitting out the red and black button as if
it were a real body part. The poor balding bear
was already bleeding from the mouth –
a permanent stain from the red medicine
I gave her instead of me.

Her velvet nose was threadbare from rubbing
against my own – at night when they argued,
her paws pressed over my ears and her furry chest
became the warm cave of my breathing:
safe, till morning when Mum stitched back
the eye, black and red, just like hers.

Bellybuttons

Bellybuttons are closet contortionists, yawn when we
stretch, wink as we do up shoes, yet they perform most
of their mimodramas behind a curtain of clothes, or
coyly into a mirror. The braver ones go public in
summer, busk on beaches: deep and meaningful
or pale and shy, under short shirts;
others pop out to steal the show.

Yet, the true artists outshine all the rest studded and
ringed, exotic, erotic, they jangle and dance with every
step: proud of the wound that gave them life.

It's a boy

bouton: French, a bud, knob, protuberance

The champignon
beneath the newborn's
swaddling: waiting
years under layers
of fabric leaves
to one day rise
on its stalk
to perpetuate.

Bob Ellis's top button

His white shirt, once lovingly ironed
by a wife a thousand miles away
is now dishevelled like his hair,
the top button straining at his neck.
Tie askew, he's Les Patterson slouching
in the queue for a burger
with sauce that's bound to land
somewhere between his braces.

While he's being served,
this button's had enough and dives off
into a tub of lettuce beside the bench.
Bob doesn't blink, safety laws
don't cross his mind as he strolls out
of the 'Beer and Burger' tent, fly half undone,
not a thought about the poor sod
who'll get a button in their bun.

When Piggy caught his lily

Piggy caught his lily in the zip,
dear old Aunt Jean reported
down the telephone line,
came home sozzled,
had a back lawn tinkle and
forgot to put his lily away.

For years there were stories
of wincing doctors
and nimble-fingered nurses
easing out each trapped fold
from zipper teeth – thirty-two
tweezerings all in all.

And cousin Piggy still
warns partygoers to this day to
never close the roller door before
putting the block and tackle away
while wise Aunt Jean replies
on the virtues of button-up flies.

by Jude	**by Joan**
Mother's collection	At our fingertips
How do fingers sense	Sacred
Seamstress	Spare buttons
Haberdashery dreaming	Beginner
Climbing back	In the light
Buttoned against sin	A common thread
Nipples	From her lover's uniform
Love's promise	The Coles Girl
Haiku	Stories from remnants
Deep in a forest	Memento
In shadows	I heard a strange tale…
Don't curse your cardie	Museum of Lost Buttons
The fat aftermath	Relic of faith
Lunar cat	Still life
the button that has…	Boutons fantaisie
Famous buttons	Enigma
Bizarre buttons	Puppeteer
A lady's cuffs	Together
Might come in handy	Ruby's red coat
Broken toys	
Bellybuttons	
It's a boy	
Bob Ellis's top button	
When Piggy caught his lily	

Acknowledgements

Jude

Mother's collection – *On a moon spiced night*, Wakefield Press, 2004

Nipples – *WomanSpeak*, Wakefield Press, 2009

Deep in a forest – *Short & Twisted*, 2011; *Ripples Magazine*, Issue 20, 2011

The fat aftermath – *Midnight Echo*, 2010; performed at Adelaide Festival of Ideas, 2011; on University of Oxford website (Science and Ethics), 2011

Bellybuttons – *Knifing the Ice*, Wakefield Press, 2000

Dark buttons – *Ripples Magazine*, Issue 20, 2011

I thank the universe for giving us the simple pleasures of poetry and buttons – and I thank my family and friends who are like diamond buttons, fastened to my past and future. I also thank the worldwide community of button collectors for being as crazy as Joan and I. I am, therefore I collect. Thank you Ginninderra Press for supporting poetry; and Sarah for capturing our poems in her illustrations. And a special thank you to my daughter Jasmine for giving me a button-encrusted notebook, thus beginning my button jottings – and to Joan for joining me on the laughter-filled journey to *Thread Me a Button*.

Joan

Ruby's Red Coat, In the Light – *Marilyn Monroe by the Brooklyn Bridge and other portraits*, Ginninderra Press, 2009

From her lover's uniform, A common thread – *Season of a New Heart*, Effective Living Centre, 2010

The Coles Girl, *The Heart of Port Adelaide*, Ginninderra Press, 2011

Thank you to Stephen at Ginninderra Press for giving poets the chance to see their words on paper. To my family and friends – a big thank you for their love and encouragement, and especially to Peter for his unwavering support and Sarah for her stunning illustrations. A very special thank you to Jude who initiated our button journey and invited me to join her. Her encouragement and inspiration, and the fun we've had along the way, have made for an unforgettable experience.

Joan Fenney & Jude Aquilina. Photo: Robert Ramsey.

Jude Aquilina grew up in suburban Magill, then moved to the Adelaide Hills. She has published three poetry collections with Wakefield Press and edited a number of poetry anthologies. Her poems are published throughout Australia and overseas. Jude works at the SA Writers' Centre, teaches in the Professional Writing Unit at Adelaide College of the Arts and is a freelance editor. Jude is President of Adelaide PEN, an international organisation that fights for the rights and release of imprisoned writers.

Joan Fenney grew up in the foothills of Victoria's Dandenong Ranges, before moving to South Australia in the early 1980s. Joan has been a journalist for over twenty-five years. Her poetry has been published in newspapers, journals, magazines and in a number of anthologies including *Award Winning Australian Writing 2011*, *The Heart of Port Adelaide* (2011) and *Season of a New Heart* (2010). Joan's first poetry collection, *Marilyn Monroe by the Brooklyn Bridge and other Portraits*, was published by Ginninderra Press in 2009.

www.ingramcontent.com/pod-product-compliance
Lightning Source LLC
Chambersburg PA
CBHW062153100526
44589CB00014B/1822